LADYBIRD  HISTORIES

Anglo-Saxons

D1147044

3 0116 01972959 7

History consultant: Philip Parker, historian and author
Map illustrator: Martin Sanders

A catalogue record for this book is available from the British Library

Published by Ladybird Books Ltd
80 Strand, London, WC2R 0RL
A Penguin Company

001

© LADYBIRD BOOKS LTD MMXV

LADYBIRD and the device of a Ladybird are trademarks of Ladybird Books Ltd.

All rights reserved. No part of this publication may be reproduced,
stored in a retrieval system, or transmitted in any form or by any means,
electronic, mechanical, photocopying, recording or otherwise,
without the prior consent of the copyright owner.

ISBN: 978-0-72329-442-9
Printed in China

LADYBIRD HISTORIES

Anglo-Saxons

Written by Jane Bingham
Main illustrations by Giorgio Bacchin
Cartoon illustrations by Clive Goodyer

Contents

Who Were the Anglo-Saxons?

Around the year 400 CE boatloads of warriors began arriving in Britain. These warlike warriors belonged to tribes of Angles and Saxons from Germany, and Jutes from Denmark. Over the next 100 years some of the raiders settled in Britain, gradually gaining control of the south and east of the country. They became known as the Anglo-Saxons, and their country was called 'Angle-land' or England. Anglo-Saxon England lasted for around 500 years, until the Norman Conquest in 1066.

Today we think of the Anglo-Saxons as the ancestors of the English people. But when they first came to Britain they were foreign raiders.

Anglo-Saxon life

Most Anglo-Saxon people lived in small villages and worked as farmers. Some specialized in crafts, and some became traders. Boys trained as warriors and people gathered to hear stories about their brave warrior ancestors.

The first invaders were pagans who worshipped many gods. By the 800s CE most people had converted to Christianity. When the Anglo-Saxon period came to an end towns had developed, trade was growing and most people enjoyed a peaceful way of life.

How do we know?

We have plenty of evidence about the Anglo-Saxon way of life. Archaeologists have uncovered the remains of settlements and graves, finding armour, weapons, jewellery, cooking pots and tools. Anglo-Saxon monks recorded their people's history, and poems like *Beowulf* provide a vivid picture of life in Anglo-Saxon times. Some early manuscripts show scenes from daily life, while the Bayeux Tapestry tells the story of the Norman Conquest.

Before the Anglo-Saxons

When the Anglo-Saxons first arrived in Britain they discovered a land that was both Roman and Celtic. Since the Roman conquest in 43 CE, Britain had been part of the Roman Empire, and many people had adopted the Roman way of life. However, in parts of the country Britain's ancient Celtic traditions and beliefs had survived.

Roman Britain

The Romans ruled Britain for over 300 years. During that time they built villas, towns, forts and farms, which were linked by a network of roads. Under Roman rule, people in Britain worshipped Roman gods and obeyed Roman laws, and some even learned to speak Latin – the official language of Rome. Many Britons worked for the Romans, helping to run the province of Britannia.

Roman towns followed a regular plan.

Celtic Britain

Although the Romans conquered Wales and Cornwall, they did not settle there, and little of Scotland was ever part of the Roman Empire. In these regions, Celtic people lived in tribes and their culture stayed strong. Most were farmers living in small settlements round hillside forts.

Celtic settlements were built around a fort.

Scary fighters

Celtic warriors prepared for battle by covering their bodies with woad, a blue-coloured war paint. They rubbed mud into their hair to make it stand up in spikes, so they would look extra-scary!

Three cultures

Under the Anglo-Saxons a new kind of society developed, but the Celtic and Roman cultures did not disappear. Instead they combined with Anglo-Saxon customs to form an English way of life.

The Anglo-Saxons Arrive

By the 380s CE the Roman Empire was crumbling. Warrior tribes were launching attacks on many parts of the Empire, and even the city of Rome was in danger. Roman troops were called back to Rome to deal with this threat, and around the year 410 CE the last Roman soldiers left Britain.

A time of chaos

After the Romans had left, people in Britain slowly returned to their Celtic way of life, living in tribes again. Cities and towns were neglected and began to fall into ruins, and farms were abandoned. Without an organized army to defend their country, the Britons became an easy target for invaders.

A land of giants?

People in Anglo-Saxon England were amazed by the ruins of Roman cities. Many had no idea that their country had once been ruled by the Romans. Instead they believed that these huge empty buildings were the work of giants!

Invaders and settlers

With the Roman army gone, the invaders were able to take land from the Britons. They seized their chance to capture land and began to set up their own farms and villages. Most of the invaders were Angles, Saxons or Jutes, but some were Frisians from Holland.

Soldier settlers

Some Angles and Saxons who settled in Britain were not invaders. They had been invited to help defend Britain. The Romans – and later the Britons – were desperate to ward off Celtic attacks from Scotland and Ireland, so they made agreements with foreign tribes who provided soldiers to fight on their side. Afterwards, some of the Angles and Saxons stayed on and claimed British land.

Angles and Saxons launched surprise raids on Britain.

Anglo-Saxon Kingdoms

Some Britons fought fiercely against the Anglo-Saxon invaders, but their advance could not be stopped. By the 570s CE the Anglo-Saxons controlled most of the south-east. In 577 CE a warrior called Ceawlin led the West Saxons against the Britons at the Battle of Deorham, near Bath. He was victorious and many Britons were forced to retreat west. After this victory the Anglo-Saxons claimed almost all of southern Britain.

Celts and Anglo-Saxons

By the 600s CE thousands of Anglo-Saxons had settled in Britain. Some Britons were driven off their land and retreated to Scotland, Wales and Cornwall. However, not all Britons fled to these Celtic lands. Many stayed in England and accepted Anglo-Saxons as their overlords.

Some Celts fou

Anglo-Saxon land

Map of the Anglo-Saxon kingdoms.

Anglo-Saxon England was divided into several kingdoms. East Anglia was where the Angles first settled. Kent was home to the Jutes, and the Saxons claimed Wessex, Sussex and Essex. By about 650 CE the two largest kingdoms were Northumbria and Mercia.

Powerful kings

In the early 600s CE King Aethelberht of Kent was the most powerful English ruler. He helped bring Christianity to England. A century later the kings of Mercia were the dominant rulers. King Offa of Mercia led successful campaigns against the Celts in Wales and built a long ditch marking the border between England and Wales.

Walking the Dyke

Today, more than a thousand years after it was made, Offa's Dyke is used as a walking path. The track extends for 280 kilometres (175 miles).

Viking Invaders

By the end of the 700s CE most of England was at peace. Nearly four centuries had passed since the Anglo-Saxons had first invaded. Christianity had spread throughout the country and people had settled down to an 'English' way of life. But then a new threat arrived, as hordes of Viking raiders began to descend on English shores.

Raiders and settlers

In 793 CE Viking warriors landed on Lindisfarne, off the north-east coast of England. Lindisfarne was home to a Christian monastery with many fine treasures. The raiders seized its riches and slaughtered most of its monks, before sailing away again to sea. Over the next few years the Vikings also raided the monasteries of Iona and Jarrow, and were soon launching attacks every year. After 850 CE the Vikings stayed over the winter, and the raids continued throughout the year.

A Danish invasion

In 865 CE the Vikings launched an invasion of England. The invaders were a large force of Danish soldiers, known to the English as the 'Great Army'. They first landed in East Anglia, and slaughtered many people, before spreading outwards. In 866 CE they captured York, and over the next three years they won control of Northumbria, East Anglia and Mercia. By 870 CE it seemed the Anglo-Saxons were facing total defeat.

Who were the Vikings?

The Vikings came from Denmark, Norway and Sweden. There they were farmers, hunters and fishermen, although they also trained as warriors and sailors. Some worked as merchants, metalworkers, carpenters, poets and musicians. But they are best known today for their raids – a series of armed invasions along the coast of Europe that lasted from around 800 to 1000 CE.

Viking raiders terrified the monks of Lindisfarne.

King Alfred the Great

In 870 CE the Danish army launched an attack on Wessex. The West Saxons fought back fiercely, but failed to stop the Danes. When Alfred became king of Wessex in 871 CE he inherited a kingdom that was in danger of being overrun by the Danes.

The Battle of Edington

King Alfred was forced to spend two years of his reign in the marshes of Somerset. From there he planned attacks on the Danish forces, and led a series of raids against them. In 878 CE Alfred and his army finally defeated the Danes at the Battle of Edington. This victory stopped the Danish advance through Anglo-Saxon lands. The Danes made peace with the Anglo-Saxons, and their leader, King Guthrum, agreed to become a Christian.

Dividing England

In 886 CE Alfred and Guthrum made an important treaty. England was divided in two, with the north and east ruled by the Danes, while Alfred was king in the south and west. Each half had its own laws, and the part under Danish rule became known as the 'Danelaw'.

Map of England in 886 CE.

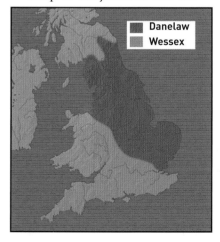

Danelaw
Wessex

King Alfred made sure his kingdom was well defended from raiders.

A great ruler

King Alfred brought peace and wealth to his kingdom. He built a series of forts to defend his land from attack, and set up a navy to fight off invasions by sea. He also encouraged religion and learning, and organized the translation of many books from Latin into Anglo-Saxon.

Alfred and the cakes

A story is told about King Alfred when he was living in the marshes. In the story, he was left in charge of a woman's cakes, but was so busy plotting to defeat the Danes that he let them burn. The woman was angry, not realizing he was her king, and that he would soon lead her people to victory!

England Unites

England was divided for almost seventy years. During this time many people from Denmark and Norway settled in the Danelaw in north-east England. But some Anglo-Saxons were determined to win back their land.

The first English king

In 924 CE Alfred's grandson Aethelstan became the new ruler of the Anglo-Saxons. He won the Battle of Brunanburh in 937 CE, driving the Danes from their English lands. This victory made him the first king of all England. Aethelstan established a single set of laws for the whole kingdom, but still struggled against the Vikings. Soon after their defeat at Brunanburh the Danes recaptured York, but in 954 CE they were thrown out of England.

Aethelstan won a great victory at the battle of Brunanburh.

Aethelred and the Danegeld

Aethelstan's descendants ruled as kings of England, although they still had to fight off Danish attacks. In 978 CE ten-year-old Aethelred inherited the throne and was faced with a new wave of raids. Following his defeat at the Battle of Maldon in 991 CE, Aethelred collected large sums of money, known as Danegeld, which he paid to the Danes to keep them away. But this did not work for long and in 992 CE the raids began again.

Aethelred's revenge

In 1002 CE Aethelred decided to take revenge on the Vikings. He ordered that all Danish men living in England should be put to death. It is not known how many Danes were killed, but the massacre caused fury in the Viking lands. A year later King Sweyn Forkbeard of Denmark launched the first in a series of raids on the English coast.

Aethelred the Unready

Today King Aethelred is known by the nickname 'the Unready'. Many people assume he was given this title because he was not prepared for the Viking raids. In fact, the name is a misunderstanding of his Anglo-Saxon nickname, which meant 'the badly advised'. He was called this because he did not surround himself with wise people and made some foolish decisions.

Danish and English Kings

In 1013 CE King Sweyn Forkbeard of Denmark invaded England. Danish troops landed in East Anglia and advanced through the country, claiming land as they went. Aethelred and his sons fled abroad, and Sweyn was crowned on Christmas Day. However, his reign was very short. Just five weeks later he died after falling from his horse.

King Cnut

 After Sweyn's death the English throne returned to Aethelred and then to his son. But in 1015 CE, Sweyn's son Cnut invaded England. In October 1016 CE Cnut won a decisive victory and one month later he became king of England.

Cnut ruled England for almost twenty years until his death in 1035 CE. He was a wise ruler, encouraging trade and supporting the Church, and he gained the trust of the English by sending home most of his Danish army and relying on English advisers. During his reign Cnut also became king of Denmark, Norway and parts of Sweden.

Edward the Confessor

After Cnut's death England was ruled by his sons Harold Harefoot and Harthacnut. But when Harthacnut died in 1042 CE there was no obvious Danish ruler to take over.

Instead, the Anglo-Saxons chose Edward, son of King Aethelred (see page 19). After twenty-seven years of Danish kings, England had an Anglo-Saxon king once more. King Edward was crowned in 1043 CE. His first task was to gain control of the English nobles, and he also had to fight off Celtic raiders from Scotland and Wales. But he was not a strong ruler. When he died without an heir in 1066 CE England faced an uncertain future.

Edward the Confessor

After his death King Edward was made a saint and given the title 'Edward the Confessor'. Confessor was a name given to holy people who spent a lot of time praying and who lived a virtuous life.

King Edward was a devout Christian who paid for the building of Westminster Abbey in London.

Anglo-Saxon Society

Anglo-Saxon society was divided into four main classes. At its head was the king, and under him were the nobles, known as thanes. The largest group were free people, or churls, but there were also many slaves. Most people lived in villages on estates that were ruled by thanes, but by the end of the Anglo-Saxon period some villages had grown into towns.

Thanes

The thane lived in a large hall in the centre of the village. He owned all the land round the village and all the animals that grazed there. If he wanted to go to war, he could call on the village men to fight for him. In return he protected the villagers.

Churls

Churls worked on the thane's land and looked after his animals. As well as working for the thane, each churl family had a few strips of land to farm. Male churls swore loyalty to their thane and promised to fight for him in times of war.

Slaves

Slaves had very few rights and were entirely owned by their masters and mistresses. Sometimes very poor people sold themselves or their children into slavery in order to survive. But many slaves were Celts, who had been captured as prisoners of war.

Earls and sheriffs

In the early Anglo-Saxon period England had many kings who each ruled small kingdoms, but after 937 CE it was mainly ruled by one king. In 1017 CE King Cnut divided England into four earldoms. Each region was governed by an earl and was split into smaller units called shires. The shires were governed by 'shire reeves', who soon became known as sheriffs.

Sheriffs settled legal disputes in the villages.

The Witan

Around the year 600 CE Anglo-Saxon kings began to hold meetings with the Witan. This was a group of powerful nobles who advised the king. The Witan also had to choose a new king if there were rival claims to the throne.

Village Life

Most Anglo-Saxon people lived in villages. Their houses were grouped round the thane's hall and surrounded by land. Cows and sheep grazed in the fields, while pigs and chickens were kept nearer the houses. In the heart of the village was a weaving shed and a large oven for baking bread.

Village homes

Churls and their families lived in simple one-roomed homes. Their houses were made from planks of wood, with thatched roofs made from straw or reeds. Inside the main room was a fireplace with a metal cooking pot hanging over it. People sat and slept on benches, and stored their few possessions in wooden chests. Most homes had no windows and just a small hole in the roof above the fire, so they were dark and smoky.

People of all ages lived together in an Anglo-Saxon home.

Work for all

People were kept busy working on the thane's land and looking after his animals, but they still found some time for other activities. Men and boys went hunting and fishing for extra food. They also trained as warriors, so they would be ready to fight when needed.

Women did most of the cooking and looked after the children. They worked in the weaving sheds, where they spun wool from the village sheep and wove the thread into clothes, blankets and wall hangings.

Children helped their parents in order to learn the skills they would need for adult life. Boys practised hunting and fighting, while girls were taught to cook and weave.

Marrying young

The Anglo-Saxons got married very young. Brides were usually about twelve years old and grooms were around fourteen. The groom was expected to pay a 'bride price' to the father of his bride. The payment could be in money, cattle, labour or goods.

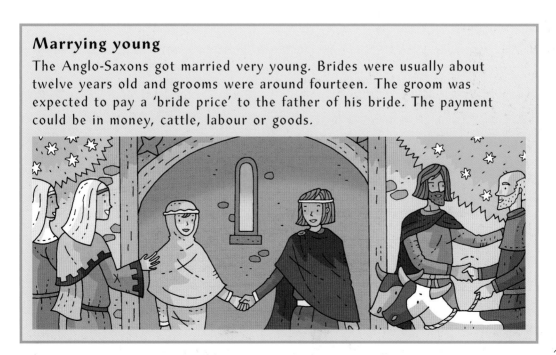

Farming

The Anglo-Saxons grew crops, vegetables and some fruit. Wheat and rye were used for bread. Barley was used for brewing beer, and oats were made into porridge. Carrots, parsnips, cabbages, peas, beans and onions were grown in fields and vegetable gardens. Fruit trees produced apples, pears, plums and cherries.

Farm animals

Pigs were reared for their meat, while cows were mainly kept for their milk, which was also made into cheese. Sheep provided wool, as well as milk for cheese, and chickens supplied eggs.

When an animal was no longer useful it was killed and eaten. People made sure that no part was wasted. Skins were turned into leather, hooves were boiled to make glue, and animal fat was used to make oil for lamps.

Different jobs

Men and boys worked in the fields, ploughing, planting and harvesting. They led teams of oxen, dragging heavy wooden ploughs through the earth, while smaller children scared away birds. Cowherds and shepherds watched over animals, making sure they were safe from wolves. Women and girls fed the pigs and chickens, milked the cows and made cheese.

Keeping bees

There was no sugar in Anglo-Saxon England, so honey was precious. Villagers kept bees in wicker hives, and used their honey to sweeten food and to make an alcoholic drink called mead.

The thane's hall stood in the centre of a farming village.

Food and Feasting

Most Anglo-Saxon people ate food they had grown themselves. This meant they had a basic diet of bread, porridge and vegetable stews. Meals were sometimes varied with eggs, cheese or milk, or with a little meat or fish. People also gathered the berries, fruit and nuts that grew wild.

Fishing and hunting

Men and boys went fishing in their local rivers and streams. If they were close to the coast, they could also gather oysters, cockles, crabs and mussels. Hunters set traps for wild birds, hares and other small creatures. Sometimes the villagers went hunting for larger animals, but forests were often controlled by nobles, who enjoyed the sport of hunting.

People fished and hunted with lines, spears, nets and traps.

Village feasts

On special occasions, such as harvest-time, the thane held a feast for the whole village in his hall. Pigs were roasted on the village spit, and there was plenty of bread, ale and mead.

Ale for all

People of all ages drank watery ale made from barley. Ale was considered much safer to drink than water from rivers or ponds.

Special feasts

Sometimes, kings and earls held grand Anglo-Saxon feasts, serving roast venison and boar, delicious pies and pastries and fine wine. Guests ate from silver platters and drank from decorated drinking horns. Musicians played harps and pipes, and storytellers called scops recited poems about battles and heroes.

Guests were entertained as they ate and the feasts lasted for many hours.

Clothes and Jewellery

Poor people's clothes were made from rough woollen cloth that had been spun and woven in village weaving sheds. Garments for wealthy men and women were made from the finest wool, linen or silk. Clothes were dyed using pigments made from plants and rocks, and they often had colourful woven strips sewn along their borders.

The most common colours were green, yellow, orange and brown. Scarlet and blue dyes were expensive so they were only used by the rich.

Men and boys

Men and boys wore a simple tunic with a belt. In winter they added thick cloaks and loose trousers, and sometimes used leather strips to bind their trousers to their legs. Working men wore short tunics, but wealthy men and boys displayed their higher status by wearing longer tunics.

Women and girls

Women and girls wore a long-sleeved under-dress and an outer-dress rather like a pinafore. They often covered their head with a scarf and in winter they wore a thick shawl that was fastened to their dress with two brooches.

Shoes

Most people wore very simple shoes that were usually made from a single piece of leather. Wealthy people wore more delicate, pointed shoes.

Jewellery and charms

Poor men and women fastened their cloaks with metal pins or bronze brooches, while wealthy people used elaborate brooches made from silver and gold. Rich women wore jewellery made from precious metals, ivory and amber. Less wealthy women made simple necklaces from pieces of stone, shell and bone.

Many adults and children wore amulets round their necks. Amulets were stones, teeth or carvings that were believed to have magic powers. People believed they would keep them safe.

jewellery

brooch

amulet

Sports and Games

The Anglo-Saxons worked hard, but they knew how to enjoy themselves, too. They took part in boisterous outdoor sports and also played indoor games. Children joined in the fun inside and out, and played with simple hand-made toys.

Outdoor sports

Men and boys tested their strength by wrestling and weight-lifting. They held competitions to see who could jump the highest and the furthest, and who could stay under water the longest. Sometimes they formed two teams to play rowdy ball games rather like modern hockey and baseball, and competed against each other in running, swimming, rock-climbing and horse-riding.

Sometimes men held contests to see who could lift the heaviest rock.

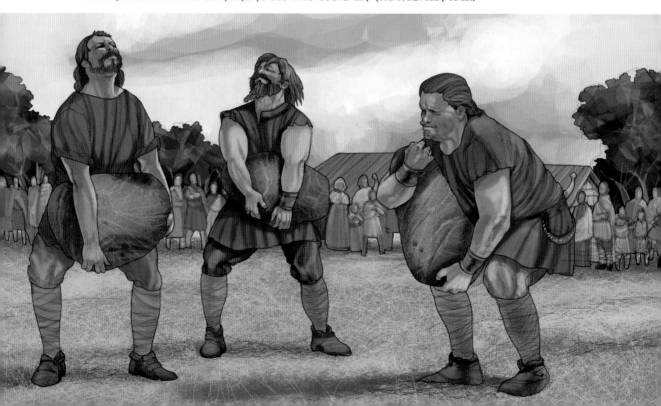

Drowning allowed!

In an Anglo-Saxon swimming race it was considered perfectly fair to push your rivals under the water and try to drown them!

Tug-of-war

Sometimes teams of villagers held a tug-of-war. Each team pulled the opposite end of a rope made from animal skin. The aim was to see which team was the strongest. The contest was often held over a fire to add an extra element of danger!

Indoor games and children's toys

In the long, dark evenings people gathered round fires to play games and test each other's wits with riddles. Board games were home-made, with wooden boards, counters made of stone or wood, and dice carved from deer antlers.

Girls and boys played with wooden animals, boats and spinning tops. Girls had dolls made from wood and cloth, and boys had wooden swords. Older children played a game called 'knuckles', using just one hand to pick up small stones as quickly as they could.

Warriors and Warfare

Anglo-Saxon men had to be prepared to fight at any time. If an enemy attacked, thanes fought for their king, and churls fought for their thane. Boys began training for battle when they were young and men continued to practise their fighting skills.

Training to fight

Boys practised fighting with spears, axes and javelins. They learned to use a shield to defend themselves and to shoot arrows from a bow. The sons of kings, earls and thanes trained to fight with swords, but swords were too expensive for churls.

Fathers taught their sons their fighting skills.

The Bayeux Tapestry

One source of evidence for Anglo-Saxon warfare is the Bayeux Tapestry. It was made in England in the 1070s CE and tells the story of the Norman Conquest. The tapestry shows many violent scenes from the Battle of Hastings.

Women warriors

There is evidence that women sometimes fought beside men. Alfred the Great's daughter Aethelflaed is said to have played a leading role in battles against the Vikings. Archaeologists have found the graves of female warriors, who were buried with their spears and shields.

Armour and weapons

Warriors wore pointed metal helmets, with a panel to cover the nose. They dressed in chain-mail tunics and had wooden shields that were usually round in shape.

In battle, a line of soldiers often used their shields to form a wall to protect them.

Javelins and bows and arrows were used for long-range attacks, while soldiers relied on their spears, swords and axes in the heart of battle. The most feared weapon was the two-bladed battleaxe, which could do terrible damage, sometimes splitting a man's skull in half. Swords were highly prized and usually decorated with fine carvings. Some swords even had spells carved on them to protect the sword-bearer and bring him luck in battle.

Crafts and Skills

Some villagers were expert at working with wood, metal, leather or clay. They passed their skills on to their children, and some talented men and women set up workshops.

Chain mail, buckets, pots and goblets were made by skilled craftsmen.

Metalwork

Village blacksmiths made useful objects from iron, such as horseshoes, tools and cooking pots. Skilled metalworkers worked in precious metals, making jewellery, armour and weapons, bowls, jugs and cups. These beautiful objects were decorated with swirling patterns and often inlaid with jewels.

Antlers and horns

Antlers and horns were never wasted. Bone from a deer's antlers was made into beads, buckles, combs and knife handles. Horns from cattle were used as drinking cups. Pieces of horn were pressed flat and split into sheets to be used in lanterns.

Wood, leather and pottery

Carpenters made chests, benches and tables, as well as larger items, such as looms, ploughs and wagons. Woodturners used a machine called a pole lathe to shape wooden cups and bowls. Leatherworkers made shoes, bags and belts, and saddles and bridles for horses. Potters made bowls, jugs and cups, and decorated their work with geometric patterns.

Weaving

All village women learned to spin and weave, using wool from local sheep, and some expert weavers were employed by kings, nobles and bishops to weave clothes from linen or silk. These fine garments were embroidered, often with gold and silver thread. By the end of the Anglo-Saxon period English needlework was famous throughout Europe, where it was known as 'Opus Anglicanum' or 'English work'.

Religion and Beliefs

The Anglo-Saxons who arrived in Britain in the 400s CE worshipped many gods and goddesses. They held open-air ceremonies, and made sacrifices to their gods in return for their help and protection. These beliefs and practices were widespread in England until the 600s CE when Christianity began to spread through the country. Within a century the religion of the Anglo-Saxons had almost completely died out.

Gods and goddesses

The chief Anglo-Saxon god was Woden. He was the god of wisdom and ruled over the Next World. Other important gods were Thunor, the god of thunder, Frige, the goddess of love, and Tiw, the god of war. People made offerings to household gods called Cofgodas, who were seen as protectors of the family home.

Woden had four magical creatures to serve him. Two wolves fought for him and two ravens brought him news from all over the universe.

Worship and sacrifice

People built temples for their gods in sacred places, such as hilltops or clearings in woods. These temples were usually made from wood and contained large statues of the gods. Ceremonies were held in the temples and animals, such as oxen, were sacrificed to the gods. People believed that these gifts would keep the gods happy and encourage them to help people on Earth.

Northern gods

Anglo-Saxon beliefs came from the religions of northern Germany and Scandinavia. This meant the Anglo-Saxon gods were similar to the Viking gods. For example, the Vikings' chief god Odin resembles Woden, and the Vikings' Thor is very like Thunor.

Supernatural spirits

To the early Anglo-Saxons, the world seemed full of magical spirits, and most of them were frightening. Elves and dwarves were mischief-makers, while giants and dragons brought death and destruction. People told stories about the tricks, plots and battles of these mysterious beings.

Death and Burial

Before the spread of Christianity people believed that the dead travelled to the Next World to live with the gods. They buried their relatives with all the things they would need to enjoy life after death.

Ready for the Next World

Men were usually buried with their tools and weapons. Women often had a cooking pot and spoon, a spindle for spinning wool, a comb and some jewellery. Wealthy women were buried with large amounts of jewellery, while rich men had armour and weapons, cattle and horses. Sometimes slaves were killed and buried with their master so that they could serve him after death.

Food for the journey

In many graves a small amount of food and drink was placed beside the dead person. People believed that the dead would need a meal before they made their journey to the Next World.

Ship burials

Some important warriors were buried in ships. A fascinating example of a ship burial was discovered in Sutton Hoo in Suffolk. Inside an upturned warship were the remains of a decorated helmet, a sword and shield, and some fine ornaments. There were also useful items, such as bowls, spoons and cups. Often a burial ship was simply covered with earth, as it was at Sutton Hoo, but sometimes it was set on fire and pushed out to sea.

Cremations

Some people were cremated rather than being buried. The Anglo-Saxon poem *Beowulf*, which was composed some time between the 500s and 1000s CE, has a dramatic description of the hero's cremation. The poet describes how Beowulf's followers built an enormous bonfire and laid his body on it, surrounded by his weapons and armour. After the body had been burned the hero's ashes and many treasures were covered by a mound of earth.

Warriors were often given ship burials.

Medicine and Magic

There were no trained doctors in Anglo-Saxon England, although some people specialized in treating diseases. A few educated men studied Greek and Roman medicine, but most healers relied on traditional knowledge. If their cures failed to work, they turned to spells and prayers.

Herbs and medicines

Healers made medicines and ointments from herbs and plants, which they sometimes mixed with other ingredients. For example, an ointment made from stinging nettles was used to ease muscle pain, while lichen was placed on wounds as a dressing. A traditional cure for a stye was a mixture of leeks, garlic and wine added to liquid from a bull's stomach.

Surgery and bloodletting

Some healers performed simple surgery. They lanced boils, amputated limbs and sewed up wounds using silk thread. They also practised bloodletting – draining blood from their patients. If a patient became very weak, healers used horse dung to stop the bleeding.

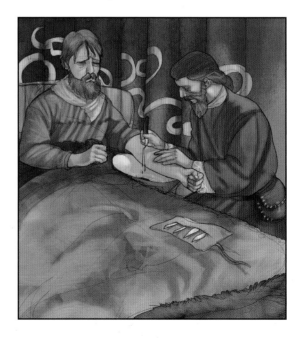

Spells and prayers

Many people believed that magic rhymes could protect them from sickness. Pregnant women were told to go to a dead man's grave and step over it three times while repeating some special words. It was believed this spell would guarantee a healthy baby.

Nasty ointments
Some of the ingredients used by healers were not very pleasant. There are recipes for ointments containing spit, urine, snails, worms and ants!

After Christianity arrived in England people began to pray to the saints for cures. It was generally believed that the relics of saints (such as their bones or teeth) had healing powers.

Some people went on pilgrimages to pray at shrines where saints' relics were kept.

43

The Coming of Christianity

When the Anglo-Saxons first arrived in Britain they found many Christian monasteries and churches. Within a century, however, most signs of Christianity had vanished. In the 500s CE many people in England worshipped the Anglo-Saxon gods (see page 38), although Christianity continued to thrive in Scotland and Wales.

Gregory and Augustine

In Anglo-Saxon times all Christians belonged to the Roman Catholic Church, which was led by the Pope in Rome. Pope Gregory I was keen that the English people should become Christians, so he sent a monk, called Augustine, to convert them. Augustine sailed to England with a group of monks, and in 597 CE he arrived on the Isle of Thanet, off the coast of Kent.

Angels not Angles

A story is told about when Pope Gregory I first saw Anglo-Saxons. As the Pope walked through a market in Rome he noticed some fair-haired prisoners of war. When told they were Angles he said, 'Not Angles, but angels!' and vowed that all Angles should be converted.

King Aethelberht's conversion

King Aethelberht of Kent travelled to Thanet to listen to Augustine. He was so impressed by what he heard that he allowed Augustine and his monks to live and preach in Canterbury. It wasn't long before Aethelberht was baptised as a Christian. He insisted his subjects follow his example. Augustine became the first archbishop of Canterbury, and founded Canterbury Cathedral.

On Christmas Day 597 CE Augustine held a baptism for thousands of people.

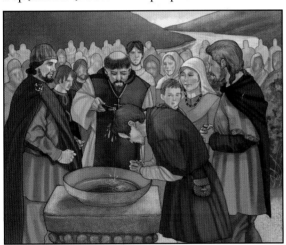

Christianity spreads

Augustine was joined by many more monks from Rome, who travelled across England, teaching the Christian message and building churches. After his death Augustine was made into a saint.

Bertha the Christian

Queen Bertha of Kent played a key part in the conversion of the Anglo-Saxons. She had been brought up in France and was a Christian when she and King Aethelberht married. Bertha persuaded her husband to welcome Augustine and later helped him to rule as a Christian king.

A Christian Country

As monks from Rome were converting the people of southern England, Celtic missionaries from Scotland, Ireland and Wales were preaching to the English in the north. At first there were quarrels between the Roman and Celtic churches, but in 664 CE a group of Church leaders held an important meeting. In this meeting, known as the Synod of Whitby, they agreed to form a united English Church.

Saint Cuthbert

Cuthbert was an early English saint. He spent most of his time living as a hermit in a cave. One story describes how Cuthbert prayed all night, standing up to his waist in the icy sea. When he returned to the shore a pair of otters followed him. First they panted on his feet to dry them, and then they warmed him with their fur!

The Lindisfarne Gospels

In the early 700s CE monks at Lindisfarne Abbey copied out the Gospels. They decorated their text with delicate figures and patterns, and created 'carpet pages' filled with designs. The manuscript of the *Lindisfarne Gospels* is one of the great treasures of the Anglo-Saxon age.

Monasteries and convents

By the 700s CE monasteries and convents were being founded in many parts of England. In these Christian communities monks and nuns led simple lives of work and worship. Some monks copied out Christian texts and decorated their work with patterns and pictures. These precious books are known as illuminated manuscripts.

Abbeys, cathedrals and churches

The Church in England was run by archbishops and bishops, who were in charge of abbeys and cathedrals. Then, in the 900s CE, thanes began to build small churches. Villagers gathered in parish churches for services run by priests.

During the late Anglo-Saxon period parish churches were built in almost every village.

Stories, Poems and Histories

The Anglo-Saxons were great storytellers. People told exciting tales about their warrior ancestors and scops recited poems and sang at feasts. Most of these stories have been lost, but some were written down in manuscripts.

Beowulf

The most famous Anglo-Saxon story is *Beowulf*, a long poem that describes the life and battles of a great warrior lord. The poem is divided into three sections for Beowulf's struggles with a monster named Grendel, his fight with Grendel's mother, and his final battle with a dragon that guards a hoard of treasure. Scholars think that *Beowulf* was first composed in the 500s CE and then passed down before it was finally written out in the 1000s CE. Nobody knows who wrote it.

Beowulf fighting Grendel, the monster.

Bede

Bede was a monk and a scholar, born in 673 CE. His writings covered a wide range of subjects, including religion, history, science, medicine and astronomy. His most famous work is *History of the English Church and People*, which tells the history of England. It begins with the Roman invasions and ends with the conversion of the Anglo-Saxons to Christianity.

Caedmon

Caedmon lived in the 600s CE and is the first known English poet. Bede describes how Caedmon fell asleep while looking after some animals. He dreamed he heard a wonderful song, and when he woke up he wrote it down. Caedmon went on to compose many songs and poems about God's creation.

A sparrow in the hall

Bede used words to create some beautiful pictures. He compared our human life to the flight of a sparrow through a feasting hall. The sparrow flies into the hall from the dark night. For a short while it experiences warmth, cheerfulness and light. Then it flies out into the dark again.

The End of the Anglo-Saxons

In January 1066 CE King Edward the Confessor died without any children to succeed him. Harold Godwinson, the powerful earl of Wessex, was crowned king of England, but two other men also claimed the right to rule. William, Duke of Normandy, insisted that King Edward had chosen him as the next king but the king of Norway, Harald Hardrada, argued that Harthacnut (see page 20) had promised the English crown to the Norwegian kings.

Invasion from the north

In early September 1066 CE Harald Hardrada landed on the north-east coast of England. He was joined by Tostig, King Harold's ambitious brother, and they beat the king's troops at the Battle of Fulford. King Harold marched north to fight Harald and Tostig, and he was victorious at Stamford Bridge.

Invasion from the south

Harald Hardrada was killed at Stamford Bridge, and the threat from Norway was overcome, but King Harold had no time to relax. Eight days after his victory in the north Harold received the news that Duke William and his army had landed on the south coast. Harold's exhausted army had to march south to face the Normans.

The Battle of Hastings

King Harold and his army arrived in Hastings on 14 October 1066 CE. The Normans had advanced to meet him and fighting began around 9 a.m. Towards the end of the day Harold was killed and many of his men fled from the battleground. By night it was clear that the Normans had won.

How did Harold die?

It is generally believed that King Harold was killed by an arrow in his eye. The evidence for this comes from the Bayeux Tapestry (see page 34). In it the name 'Harold' is above a figure with an arrow in his eye, but nobody can be sure that this shows the king.

The Battle of Hastings ended in defeat for the Anglo-Saxons.

After the Anglo-Saxons

Duke William was crowned king of England on Christmas Day 1066 CE. At first he faced many rebellions from Anglo-Saxon leaders, but he soon gained control. He gave English lands to his Norman nobles, who built large castles on their estates to show they were in charge. By the 1070s CE King William was secure on the throne.

King William I was the first Norman ruler of England.

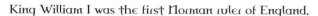

Changes in society

The Normans brought the French language and new laws to England, but life did not change much for the average villager. English peasants still worked on the land of their local lord, although he was now a French-speaking Norman. However, the Anglo-Saxon practice of keeping slaves began to disappear around the time of the Conquest.

Changes in the landscape

As the Normans gradually took control of England the English landscape began to change. The castles built by the Norman lords dominated the surrounding countryside and the Normans also built churches, monasteries and cathedrals.

Anglo-Saxon churches were generally tall and rectangular, with narrow doorways and high slit-like windows.

Norman churches were larger in scale, with rounded arches, windows and doors.

Two languages

After the Norman Conquest French was spoken by the ruling class, and many French words found their way into the English language. Today English speakers can often choose from two words with the same meaning. One word comes from the Anglo-Saxons and one comes from the Normans.

Anglo-Saxon	Norman
ask	enquire
help	aid
forgive	pardon
weird	strange
buy	purchase
freedom	liberty

What the Anglo-Saxons Did for Us

The Norman Conquest of England ended Anglo-Saxon rule, but Anglo-Saxon culture continued to play a vital part in English life. Even today the influence of the Anglo-Saxons can be seen in Britain and across the world.

Words

We use Anglo-Saxon words almost every time we speak. Most of our common words (such as 'a', 'the', 'is' and 'you') have Anglo-Saxon origins. Other common Anglo-Saxon words are 'field', 'street', 'house' and 'wood'. The Anglo-Saxons also gave us the words 'English' and 'England'.

Places

England is full of places that were named by the Anglo-Saxons. Places that end in 'ton' or 'ham' were Anglo-Saxon villages. The ending 'barrow' meant a wood, 'ford' was a river crossing and 'stow' was a meeting place.

Names

Many English surnames have their roots in Anglo-Saxon job descriptions. Some are easy to recognize, such as Baker, Brewer and Miller, but others are harder to work out.

Chapman – a shop-keeper
Cooper – a barrel-maker
Smith – a blacksmith or metalworker
Tanner – a leather-maker
Ward – a watchman
Wright – a woodworker or carpenter

The Lord of the Rings

Without the Anglo-Saxons, there would be no *Hobbit* or *Lord of the Rings*! Their author, J. R. R. Tolkien, was a professor of Anglo-Saxon and was inspired by *Beowulf* and other poems. Tolkien uses many Anglo-Saxon names and words, and his stories are filled with warriors, dwarves and dragons, just like the Anglo-Saxon legends and poems.

The adventures of Tolkien's books were inspired by Anglo-Saxon stories.

Who's Who?

Queen Bertha of Kent (539–c. 612 CE)

Bertha was the daughter of Charibert, king of the Franks, and was brought up as a Christian in France. She married King Aethelberht of Kent on the condition that she could continue to practise her religion. When Augustine arrived in Kent to preach she encouraged her husband to welcome him, and she helped to found Canterbury Cathedral and the monastery attached to it.

Saint Cuthbert (c.635–687 CE)

Cuthbert grew up near Melrose Abbey in the Anglo-Saxon kingdom of Northumbria. As a young man he did some military service before becoming a monk. He spent some time at Ripon before returning to Melrose Abbey and then went to Lindisfarne Abbey on the Farne Islands. In 685 CE Cuthbert was made bishop of Lindisfarne, but in 687 CE he resigned from this position to devote himself to prayer.

The Venerable Bede (c.673–735 CE)

Bede grew up in the Anglo-Saxon kingdom of Northumbria. At the age of seven he was sent to Monkwearmouth Abbey. When he was ten, he moved to the nearby monastery at Jarrow, where he spent the rest of his life studying and writing. Bede wrote on history, nature, astronomy, music and poetry. His most famous work was his *History of the English Church and People*.

King Offa of Mercia (c.730–796 CE)

Offa was crowned king of Mercia in 757 CE. In the next few years he became overlord of the people of Kent and Sussex, and by the 780s CE he controlled all the rulers of southern England, except those of Wessex and Northumbria. Offa fought many battles against the Welsh and built Offa's Dyke, a ditch that runs along the border between England and Wales.

King Alfred the Great (849–899 CE)

Alfred was born at Wantage in Oxfordshire. He became king of Wessex in 871 CE and in 878 CE he led the West Saxons in a great victory against the Danes at the Battle of Edington. This resulted in the division of England into English and Danish territory. Alfred ruled western England for almost 20 years. He reorganized his army, built a series of forts and established a set of laws for his kingdom.

King Aethelstan (c.893–939 CE)

Aethelstan was the grandson of Alfred the Great. He became king of the Anglo-Saxons in 924 CE. In 927 CE he conquered York, the last Viking stronghold, making him the first Anglo-Saxon ruler of the whole of England. In 937 CE he won another victory against the Danes at the Battle of Brunanburh. He created new laws, reformed English currency and encouraged trade.

King Aethelred II (c.968–1016 CE)

Aethelred became king of England at the age of ten. For much of his reign he faced attacks from the Danes. In 991 CE he began paying the Danegeld to persuade the Danes to stay away, but this did not work for long. In 1013 CE King Sweyn Forkbeard of Denmark invaded England and Aethelred fled to Normandy. Aethelred returned to rule after Sweyn's death in 1014 CE, but died in 1016 CE.

King Edward the Confessor (c.1002–1066 CE)

Edward was the son of King Aethelred II. Until he was about 40 years old he spent most of his time in exile in France. Edward was crowned king of England in 1042 CE. English trade prospered during Edward's reign, but he had to fight off raids by the Scots and Welsh and the nobles grew dangerously strong. Edward was a deeply religious man and he founded Westminster Abbey.

Timeline

380s CE   The Romans start to lose control of Britain and foreign raids on the British coast increase

400s CE   Boatloads of Angles, Saxons and Jutes arrive on British shores

c.410 CE   The last Roman soldiers leave Britain

550s CE   Angles, Saxons and Jutes create several kingdoms in southern England

577 CE   Ceawlin and the West Saxons defeat the Britons at the Battle of Deorham. Many Britons retreat westward

597 CE   Augustine arrives in Kent. This marks the start of the conversion of the Anglo-Saxons to Christianity

627 CE   King Edwin of Northumbria becomes the first Christian king in the north of England when he converts to Christianity

664 CE   Church leaders hold the Synod of Whitby, in which they agree to form a united English Church

685 CE   Cuthbert becomes bishop of Lindisfarne Abbey

731 CE   Bede finishes his *History of the English Church and People*

757 CE   Offa becomes king of Mercia and starts to gain control over other Anglo-Saxon kingdoms

793 CE   Vikings raid Lindisfarne Abbey. This is the start of many Viking raids

865 CE   The Danish Great Army lands in England

866 CE   The Great Army captures York. Over the next three years they win control of Northumbria, East Anglia and Mercia

870 CE   The Danes launch an attack on Wessex

878 CE   King Alfred defeats the Danes at the Battle of Edington

886 CE	Alfred and Guthrum, the Danish leader, make a treaty setting the borders of lands that will become known as the Danelaw
924 CE	Aethelstan becomes king of Wessex
927 CE	King Aethelstan conquers York, the last Viking territory in England. Aethelstan becomes the first king of all England
937 CE	King Aethelstan wins the Battle of Brunanburh
954 CE	The Danes are driven out of England
991 CE	King Aethelred is defeated at the Battle of Maldon. He starts to pay Danegeld
1002 CE	Aethelred orders a massacre of Danes living in England
1013 CE	King Sweyn Forkbeard of Denmark conquers England. Aethelred and his sons escape to France. Sweyn is crowned king of England but dies soon afterwards
1014 CE	Aethelred becomes king of England again
1016 CE	King Aethelred dies, and his son Edmund Ironside becomes king of England. Cnut wins the Battle of Ashingdon and becomes king of England
1035 CE	King Cnut dies and Harold Harefoot becomes king of England
1040 CE	King Harold dies and Harthacnut becomes king of England
1042 CE	King Harthacnut dies and Edward the Confessor becomes king of England
1066 CE	King Edward dies and Harold of Wessex becomes the next English king. The Normans win the Battle of Hastings and William of Normandy claims the English throne. The Anglo-Saxon age comes to an end

Glossary

adopt to follow or take up a new way of life

Angle member of a German tribe that began to settle in England in the 500s CE

archaeologist someone who learns about the past by digging up old objects and buildings

baptise to perform a ceremony to welcome somebody into the Christian Church

bloodletting the act of draining blood from a patient to make them better

boar a wild pig

Briton a person from Britain

Celtic belonging to the Celts, a large group of warrior people who lived in tribes in many parts of Europe, but who were concentrated in Scotland, Wales, Cornwall and Brittany

ceremony a public event to celebrate a special occasion. Ceremonies are often religious

chain mail hundreds of metal rings linked together

churl a free man, woman or child in Anglo-Saxon society

conquest the act of taking over a country or place

convert to change your own or someone else's beliefs

cremate to burn a dead body until it becomes ash

culture the ideas and customs of a group of people

earl	a powerful lord in Anglo-Saxon England after about 1000 CE
embroidery	cloth with patterns or figures sewn on it
empire	a group of countries or states controlled by a single ruler
estate	a large area of land belonging to a noble
fort	a very strong building which housed soldiers and resisted attacks
heir	someone with the right to take on the title, property or land of another person after their death
hermit	someone who lives alone in order to pray and live a holy life
inherit	to receive a title, land or money from another person after their death
invasion	the act of taking over a country by force
javelin	a spear that can be thrown as a weapon
Jute	a member of a tribe from Denmark that began to settle in England in the 500s CE
Latin	the official language of the Roman Empire
loom	a piece of machinery for making cloth by weaving thread
manuscript	a hand-written book
massacre	the killing of many people
missionary	someone who travels to another country or region to teach their religion

origin	starting place or beginning
pigment	natural colour from a plant or rock
possession	something that belongs to someone
raid	a rapid surprise attack by armed warriors
relic	an item that once belonged to, or was part of, a holy person, such as bones or teeth
Saxon	a member of a German tribe that began to settle in England in the 500s CE
scop	a poet in Anglo-Saxon times. Scops recited their poems and sometimes sang them
settlement	a place where people set up homes together
slaughter	to kill in a cruel way
society	people who live together and share the same laws and customs
succeed	to take over a position or a job
tapestry	a piece of cloth with woven patterns, figures or scenes
territory	land that is ruled by someone
thane	a lord in Anglo-Saxon England
tradition	a belief or custom that is passed from one generation to the next
venison	meat from a deer

Places to Visit

Sutton Hoo ship burial site, Suffolk
The site of a major Anglo-Saxon ship burial. Visitors can tour the burial mounds and see a full-size reconstruction of the main chamber, as well as some of the treasures.

West Stow Anglo-Saxon Village, Suffolk
A reconstruction of an Anglo-Saxon village, with actors.

Bede's World, Jarrow, Tyne and Wear
A museum on the life and writings of Bede, with a reconstruction of an Anglo-Saxon settlement.

British Museum, London
Contains the world's largest collection of Anglo-Saxon objects, including the Lindisfarne Gospels.

Ashmolean Museum, Oxford
Home to the Alfred Jewel and many other Anglo-Saxon items.

Churches
Very few complete churches survive from before the Norman Conquest, although many medieval churches have Anglo-Saxon features. The churches listed below are all relatively unchanged since Anglo-Saxon times:

St Laurence's Church, Bradford on Avon, Wiltshire

St Thomas's Church, Bradwell-on-Sea, Essex

All Saints' Church, Brixworth, Northamptonshire

Escomb Saxon Church, Escomb, County Durham

Index